SURVIVOR

The Donner Party

Scott P. Werther

HIGH
interest
books

Children's Press®
A Division of Scholastic Inc.
New York/Toronto/London/Auckland/Sydney
Mexico City/New Delhi/Hong Kong
Danbury, Connecticut

Book Design: Laura Stein and Christopher Logan
Contributing Editor: Matthew Pitt
Maps: Christopher Logan

Photo Credits: Cover, pp. 4, 6, 9, 16, 30 © North Wind Pictures;
p. 11 © Corbis; p. 19 © Layne Kennedy/Corbis; Maps pp. 12, 15, 25
by Christopher Logan; p. 21 © Telegraph Colour Library/FPG;
p. 22 © Galen Rowell/Corbis; p. 27 © The Huntington Library;
pp. 29, 32, 39 © Bettmann/Corbis; p. 36 © James L. Amos/Corbis;
p. 41 © Robert Holmes/Corbis

Library of Congress Cataloging-in-Publication Data

Werther, Scott P.
    The Donner Party / Scott P. Werther.
        p. cm. — (Survivor)
    Includes bibliographical references and index.
    Summary: Describes the journey of the ill-fated Donner Party,
    ninety pioneers who became stranded in the Sierra Nevada
    Mountains in the winter of 1846–47.
        ISBN 0-516-23901-5 (lib. bdg.) — ISBN 0-516-23486-2 (pbk.)
        1. Donner Party—Juvenile literature. 2. Pioneers—
    California—Biography—Juvenile literature. [1. Donner Party.
    2. Pioneers. 3. Overland journeys to the Pacific. 4. Survival.]
    I. Title II. Series

    F868.N5 W47 2002
    979.4′03—dc21
                                        2001042100

Contents

Throughout the winter of 1846, the Donner Party huddled by the fire, struggling to survive.

Introduction

The year is 1846. You are stranded high on a snow-covered mountain. Your shelter is buried in 22 feet (6.7 m) of snow. You get in and out of the shelter through a snow tunnel. The last time you ate was two days ago. Your meal was the boiled leather of a shoe. You spend hours gathering firewood each day. You're so weak from hunger that you can only carry one piece of wood at a time. You've spent the last six months traveling over 2,000 miles (3,219 km) in search of California. You left your lifelong home to bring your family there. The town in California that you are trying to get to is less than 200 miles (322 km) away, but the snow is too deep to pull your wagons through. Everyone around you is hungry. No one has enough strength to climb down the mountain to get help. Some of your friends and loved ones have already died.

This may seem like a nightmare. However, for ninety-one brave pioneers traveling to California in 1846, it was reality. This is the story of the Donner Party's horrible ordeal.

One

Fresh Start West

The United States in 1846 was a young, growing country. There were only twenty-eight states in the Union. America was fighting a war with Mexico. At stake was a section of land that would later become states such as California and Arizona. Countless people were moving West to help fight the war and settle California. California was an excellent place to start a farm. The land was fertile and plentiful. The climate was ideal for growing crops. Winters in the East and Midwest were cold and harsh, but California winters were very mild. Many families wanted to move to this land of new opportunity.

At that time, the city farthest west in the Union was Independence, Missouri. It was about a 2,500-mile (4,023 km) journey from Independence to California. People interested in

The Donner family, like hundreds of other families, dreamed of a better life out West.

heading to California would start out in Independence. They would then set out in parties, or large groups, for the long trek west. One of these large groups was the Donner Party. The families who traveled in the Donner Party had sold most of their possessions. They were emigrants, people who leave their homes to move to another place.

The group knew the journey would not be easy. They'd have to work together to get their

Did You Know?

Each family heading to California had only one covered wagon for all of their belongings. Talk about a tight fit!

As they set out for California, the Donner Party thought that their biggest danger might be attacks by Native Americans.

wagons through difficult stretches of trail. They also had a limited amount of time to make the journey. They couldn't start until April, because the spring rainfall made the soil too muddy to pull the wagons through. Yet they had to cross the Sierra Nevada Mountains before the first snowfall. If they failed, they could be trapped for months in the heavy drifts of snow.

At the time, there were still a number of Native American tribes living in the West. Settlers thought Native Americans were dangerous and

feared them. Emigrants met many Native Americans as they crossed the uncharted West. A lot of the tribes were helpful and protected the travelers from harm. Relations between emigrants and Native Americans were sometimes so friendly that they ate breakfast together in tents. However, some Native Americans were angry that their land was being invaded. Sometimes they attacked the travelers or killed their oxen.

On May 12, 1846, nine wagons and thirty-one people left Independence to make the trip to Sutter's Fort, California. The trip was organized by James Reed and brothers George and Jacob Donner. George Donner and his wife, Tamzene, had just sold their house in Springfield, Illinois. They had over ten thousand dollars in cash with them. Tamzene hid the money by sewing it into a quilt. James Reed had failed at business. He was taking his family West so that he could make another attempt at earning a fortune. With no knowledge of the struggles they would soon face, the Donner Party set out full of hope and energy.

Emigrants packed lightly to make sure that their oxen would have enough strength to survive the journey.

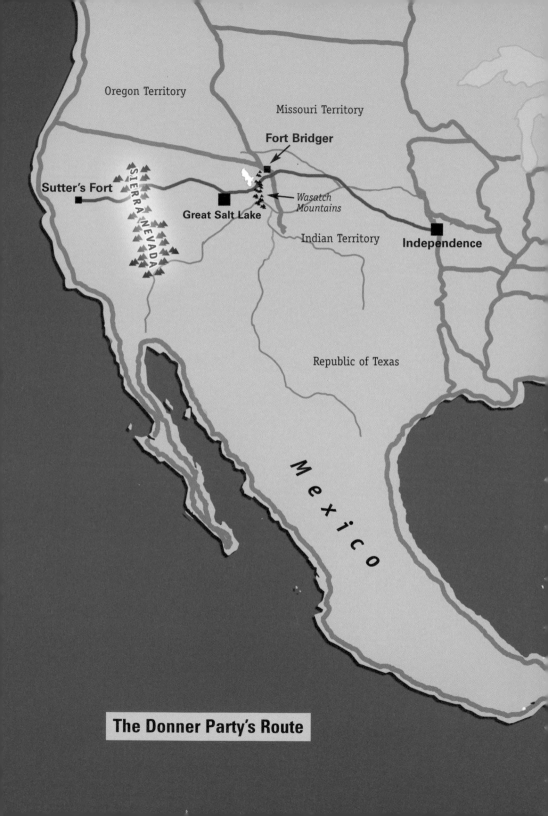

The Donner Party's Route

Two

Troubled Trail

One month into the journey, Sarah Keyes, James Reed's elderly mother-in-law, died. The harsh traveling was more than her body could take. Members of the Donner Party who survived the ordeal would later say that she was fortunate.

The Road Not Taken

Aside from Sarah's death, the journey's first half was pleasant. The wagons traveled easily across plains that would later become the states of Kansas and Wyoming. When the Donner Party reached Fort Bridger (now in Wyoming) on July 30, everyone was in good spirits. Other travelers in the area joined the Donner Party for the rest of the trip. Although these people were strangers, the Donner Party welcomed them into their group. There was safety in numbers on these long, often hazardous journeys.

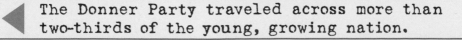

◀ The Donner Party traveled across more than two-thirds of the young, growing nation.

It was here that the Donner Party made a fatal mistake that would cost them dearly. Another emigrant named Lansford Hastings had written a book on traveling West. In it, he suggested a new way to reach California. Many wagon trains going to California that summer followed a traditional route. Hastings claimed his new route was shorter and safer. George Donner and James Reed wanted to save time. They decided to follow Hastings's shortcut. The problem was that Hastings had never even tried his own shortcut. In fact, he was on his first trip to California, too. He'd headed out West just days before the Donner Party!

The shortcut was difficult from the start. In the Wasatch Mountains (now part of Utah), the group had to clear a trail by cutting down trees. They had to pull their wagons up steep hills. This wasted valuable time. James Reed's daughter Virginia later wrote about the group's mood. "Worn with travel and greatly discouraged, we reached the shore of the Great Salt Lake. It had taken an entire month instead of a week."

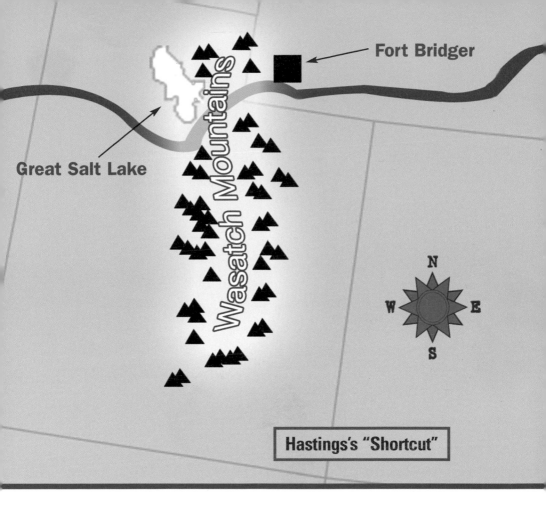

Fort Bridger

Great Salt Lake

Wasatch Mountains

N
W   E
S

Hastings's "Shortcut"

By late August, the party prepared to cross the salt flats near Utah's Great Salt Lake. The land was so dry from the sun that there was no food or water for the people or oxen. A layer of salt covered the ground. In his book, Hastings had claimed that the flats were only 40 miles (64 km) across, but they were really closer to 80 (129 km).

▲ The dry salt flats of Utah proved too much for some of the oxen.

It took the group almost a week to cross the flats. During that time, the Reeds' oxen became crazed with thirst and ran away.

Following Hastings's bad advice greatly weakened the Donner Party. The long delays and rough travel broke many people's spirits. The early autumn air hung heavy with a tense silence. People were worried that they would not reach California before the winter snows began. Their supplies were running low. As each day passed, the travelers grew more restless. Louis Keseberg put an elderly man, who was traveling with him, out of his wagon. No one else took him in. He was left on the side of the road to die.

Emotions ran high as the group pushed into territory that would someday become Nevada. In early October, James Reed got into an argument with another man. The man hit Reed on the head with the butt of his bullwhip. Reed stabbed the man, who then died. The others voted to banish Reed from the group he had helped to start. His family decided to make the rest of the journey without him. James Reed was forced to travel to Sutter's Fort alone.

Desperate Times

Two other incidents were bad omens of things to come. The first occurred days after Reed's fight. Paiute Indians crept into the camp and shot poisoned arrows at the oxen. Twenty-one oxen were killed. The Donner Party had now lost over one hundred oxen since the start of their journey.

The second incident took place later in October. As the party headed over a difficult mountain pass in the Alder Creek Valley, an axle broke on the Donner family wagon. George Donner cut his hand very badly as he was fixing the axle. There were no doctors among the group. Worse, no one had medicine to prevent a deadly infection.

Twenty-one members of the Donner Party stayed behind to help George Donner fix his wagon. The other sixty remaining members of the Donner Party continued up the mountains. They were hoping to beat the snowfall. It was now early November. The Donner Party had traveled 2,500 miles (4,023 km), enduring dangers of all kinds.

The Donners had a streak of bad luck in the fall of 1846. When George sliced his hand in October, the party had to split up.

The main group of sixty raced against time to summit the Sierra Nevada Mountains before the winter snows stopped them. Struggling to the summit, just 1,000 feet (305 m) from the peak, their greatest fear turned into a reality—the 5 feet (1.5 m) of snow at the peak would prevent them from making the crossing. There was too much snow for the oxen to trek through. They kept falling and couldn't pull the wagons. The group realized that they had reached the mountains too late. They decided to head back down the mountain to Truckee Lake and set up camp to wait out the winter snows.

The smaller Donner group never caught up with the main group. They camped in tents at Alder Creek, just 6 miles (9.7 km) east of the Truckee Lake camp. In only a few weeks, the falling snow covered the tents completely. Most of the oxen had run off or gotten lost in the snow. There was nothing to eat. People mixed the little meat they had left with anything they could chew and swallow. They ate charred bones, twigs, bark, and leaves. Meanwhile, the snow kept piling up.

Both the main group and the smaller group were in grave danger. Getting to California was no longer their major interest. Now, surviving the brutal winter was the Donner Party's only goal.

These vast, desolate salt flats sapped the strength and spirit of the Donner Party emigrants.

Three

Caught in a Nightmare

Holding Down the Fort

In Sutter's Fort, California, settlers began to get nervous. The Donner Party was the last set of emigrants expected to arrive that year and they still hadn't come. People had started to worry a month ago.

One day, late in October, James Reed had showed up, looking more dead than alive. He confirmed the fears of the Sutter's Fort settlers. The Donner Party was trapped in the mountains. The settlers at Sutter's Fort were shocked. They had thought that the emigrants had enough oxen to feed them all winter. They did not know about the losses of oxen during the Donner Party's journey.

Discovering that his family had not arrived at Sutter's Fort, James Reed was desperate to find

---

The settlers' worst fear was coming true. The group was trapped on a snow-covered mountain with the dead of winter fast approaching.

and rescue them. Because most of the men from Sutter's Fort were away fighting in the war against Mexico, few people were available to help him. Reed and another man gathered supplies and rushed to the Reed family's aid. The rain and snow drenched them mercilessly as they set out to find the group. The journey proved to be too much for the two men. They gave up their rescue attempt and headed back to Sutter's Fort. They had gotten within 12 miles (19 km) of the summit that the main group could not cross.

Self-Help

The main group at Truckee Lake and the Donner group at Alder Creek communicated with each other. People traveled back and forth bringing news from one camp to another.

In mid-December, fifteen of the strongest members from both camps set out to save themselves. The emigrants knew their chances for survival were slim. They called themselves the "Forlorn Hope." They stomped over 20-foot-high (6 m)

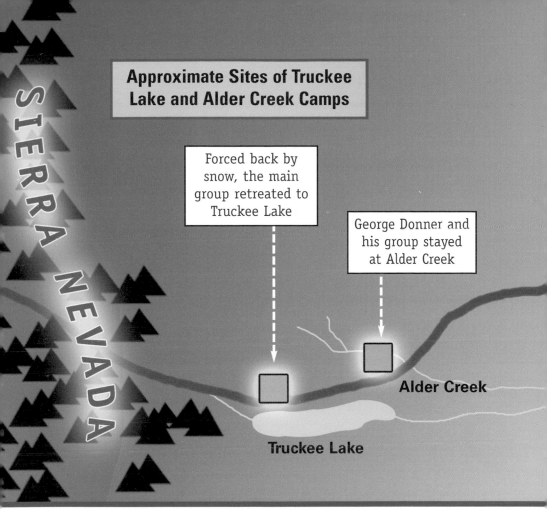

Approximate Sites of Truckee Lake and Alder Creek Camps

Forced back by snow, the main group retreated to Truckee Lake

George Donner and his group stayed at Alder Creek

Alder Creek

Truckee Lake

SIERRA NEVADA

snowdrifts. They wore homemade snowshoes made of rawhide strips and leftover pieces of wagon wood. This time they made it across the summit. It took two days to cross. The sun was so bright that the travelers could barely see. After stumbling through the snow for six days, the Forlorn

Hope group's food ran out. One of the group's members, Charles Stanton, sat in the snow—snowblind and too exhausted to go any farther. The others were too weak to help him. He was never seen again. By the ninth day, the group was hopelessly lost in the mountains. It was Christmas Eve and they hadn't eaten for days.

Desperate Measures

It started snowing again. Bad weather forced the Forlorn Hope group to set up camp. Dangerously low on supplies and with nothing left to eat, the group was desperate. They made the gruesome decision that they would have to eat someone to survive. They drew slips of paper to decide who would have to be sacrificed for the good of the group. However, no one had the heart to kill another member of the party.

As the weary, haunted travelers of the Forlorn Hope group went to sleep, the night became bitterly cold. Four people froze to death in their sleep. The survivors lit a fire to keep warm.

When William Eddy arrived at Harriet
Ritchie's house, he was at death's door.

They cut flesh from some of the dead people and cooked it. They cried as they ate the meat. But they knew that if they didn't do this, they wouldn't be able to get help for the Donner Party. The survivors would later refer to this place as "the camp of death."

On January 17, 1847, Harriet Ritchie, a woman who lived in the foothills of the Sierra Nevada Mountains, heard a knock on her door. The sight she saw when she opened the door shocked her. A frail, skeletal man asked in a faint voice if she had any bread. William Eddy from the Forlorn Hope group had finally made it to civilization. Nearby, collapsed on the trail, were six others. They were exhausted but still alive. The others hadn't been so lucky. Only seven of the fifteen Forlorn Hope members had survived.

Plea for Help

An alarm was sent out to the Californian settlers. Word was spread that many members of the Donner Party were trapped in the mountains, dying. The Californians were quick to donate money and animals. However, no one wanted to go because it was such a dangerous journey.

People soon changed their minds when they realized just how badly the Donner Party needed help. "Finally we concluded we would go or die trying, for not to make any attempt to save them would be a disgrace to us and California as long as time lasted," rescuer Daniel Rhoads later said.

The towering peaks of the Sierra Nevadas were tough for the rescue parties to cross.

The rescue party needed a few weeks to get ready. They gathered beef jerky, flour, and blankets to carry to the trapped travelers. The first relief party left on February 3, 1847. The second relief party, led by James Reed, left two days later.

Once they heard of the Donner Party's plight, the settlers of Sutter's Fort rushed to rescue their stranded friends.

Back at the Donner camp near Alder Creek, things were getting worse. George Donner's hand was dangerously infected. He barely had the strength to leave his bed. The young Donner children started to realize that their father would not survive this journey. There was hardly any food left. People were eating the animal hides they had used to make their shelters. They were boiling their shoes to eat the leather. They started to die from malnutrition, or lack of food. No one had the strength to hunt or fish. Nine long months had passed since the Donner Party left Independence, Missouri. At that time, the group was hopeful and confident. Now, most of the party did not expect to walk out of camp alive.

When the relief party first encountered the
Donner Party survivors, they were horrified
by what they saw.

Four

Delivered to Safety

By the time they crossed the summit, the first relief party was exhausted. The men were worried about what they might find. They saw nothing when they walked into the main group's camp at Truckee Lake—just a field of white. They called out.

A few bony figures slowly crawled out of holes in the snow. "Are you men from California, or do you come from heaven?" asked a horribly thin woman.

The sight of the starved people shocked the relief party. The survivors immediately begged for food. Twelve people from the main camp had died. Their bodies lay on top of the snow, covered with quilts. There were forty-eight people still alive out of the sixty. The stress had driven some people mad. Others were too close to death to be saved. However, a number of people still had enough strength to walk.

After a brief rest, the first relief party got to work. They gathered the strongest emigrants to make the journey to Sutter's Fort. Almost everyone who left at this time had to be able to walk. Many young children were left behind. The adults were too weak to carry them on the difficult journey and would have to come back for them later. There were still thirty-one people in the camp when the first relief party left on February 22. But there was hardly any food left.

As the members of the first relief party made their way through the mountains, they saw figures moving slowly in the distance. It was the second relief party led by James Reed. The first relief party had rescued James's wife Margaret and two of their children. The Reed family had not seen James in five months. Margaret Reed stumbled and almost fainted from joy when she saw her husband. The happy reunion did not last long, though. James Reed learned that two of his children were still trapped in the mountains. He pushed ahead to help them.

By the time James Reed and the second relief party reached the camp, things had gotten worse. Ten more people had died. The survivors had been forced to eat some of the dead bodies. Had they not done this, many more of them would have perished.

James Reed was happily reunited with his remaining two children. However, a storm was on the horizon. The second relief party worried that they wouldn't be able to cross the mountain if the snow continued falling. They immediately left for Sutter's Fort with a group of seventeen people.

As the group had feared, a tremendous blizzard struck before they could get across. The snow trapped them for a few days. When the storm passed, more people had died. Most of the survivors were too weak to go on. James Reed and another man were strong enough to carry the two Reed children on their backs. Another man claimed that he was strong enough to walk.

This area of the Sierra Nevadas is now known as Donner Pass, in honor of the Donner Party.

The rescuers left with only these three people. The group that stayed behind called themselves the "Starved Camp."

More Relief

A third relief party reached the Starved Camp a few days later. Some of the people had also been forced to eat the dead to stay alive. A few members of the third relief party continued on to save the emigrants still trapped on the mountain. Others stayed to take the people in the Starved Camp to safety. On March 13, the third relief party reached Alder Creek. They left the next day with four children. However, five people had to stay behind, including George Donner. He was close to death from his infected cut, so he could not make the trip. His wife Tamzene stayed with him. They said good-bye to their children for the last time. The third relief party had little trouble getting back to Sutter's Fort.

A fourth and final relief party had to wait out another month of bad weather. It was mid-April by the time they got to Alder Creek. Louis Keseberg was the only survivor of the five. He was delirious, having been trapped in the mountains for five months with barely a scrap of food. Yet he was able to make the journey across the mountain. The last of the Donner Party had finally completed the journey, ten months later.

New Beginnings

The forty-seven people who finally made it to California started new lives. They tried to carry on without the forty-four people who failed to survive the trip. This was very difficult for some. All of the Donner children were now orphans. The older girls married within a few months of reaching Sutter's Fort. Families in the region adopted the younger girls. The survivors rarely spoke of their ordeal. Emigration to California decreased after newspapers reported the Donner Party's story. People were afraid that the same thing would happen to them.

In 1848, gold was discovered in a creek near Sutter's Fort. By late 1849, the fear of crossing

Just two years after the Donner Party's fateful journey, gold was discovered near Sutter's Fort, launching the Gold Rush of 1849.

the mountains had worn off. More than 100,000 people traveled to California in search of gold. They looked in streams near the area where the Donner Party had been trapped. This area was renamed Donner Pass and Donner Lake. It became a tourist attraction.

A short time later, the first transcontinental railroad was built to connect the East and West Coasts. It went right over Donner Pass. People began to settle all over the West.

A monument was built to mark the area where so many had suffered. It stands to this day as a reminder of the great difficulties Americans faced settling their country. It honors those who paid the ultimate price chasing their dreams and those who survived one of history's greatest tragedies.

Today, curious people come from around the world to visit the site where the Donner Party suffered. This is the Donner Memorial, which pays tribute to the group's endurance and will.

VIRILE TO RISK AND
FIND: KINDLY WITHAL
AND A READY HELP
FACING THE BRUNT
OF FATE · INDOMI-
TABLE · UNAFRAID

emigrants people who leave their homes to move to another place

forlorn nearly hopeless

malnutrition a condition caused by not eating enough, or by eating unhealthy things

omen a sign of what might happen next

ordeal a very unpleasant or troubling experience

possessions things that a person owns

NEW WORDS

propose to suggest an idea or plan

reunion the act of two or more people coming together again

skeletal dangerously thin

summit the top of a mountain

territory land belonging to a group of people or a government

transcontinental stretching or going across a continent

FOR FURTHER READING

BOOKS

Boeve, Eunice. *Trapped*. New York: Royal Fireworks Press, 1995.

Calabro, Marian. *The Perilous Journey of the Donner Party*. New York: Houghton Mifflin Company, 1999.

Laurgaard, Rachel K. *Patty Reed's Doll: The Story of the Donner Party*. Sandwich, MA: Beautiful Feet Books, 1989

Lavender, David. *Snowbound: The Tragic Story of the Donner Party*. Bridgewater, NJ: Holiday House, Inc., 1996.

Web Sites

New Light on the Donner Party

http://www.utahcrossroads.org/DonnerParty/index.html

Author and historian Kristin Johnson runs this Web site. It features a timeline of the journey and helpful links to other sites.

Donner Online

http://www.kn.pacbell.com/wired/donner/

On this Web site, you can create a multimedia scrapbook about the Donner Party. You can share what you've learned by sending the link to your friends.

Donner Memorial State Park

http://www.ceres.ca.gov/sierradsp/donner.html

On this site, you can find out more about Donner Memorial State Park, Donner Lake, and the Emigrant Trail Museum. You can also plan a trip by checking schedules and current events.

Across the Plains in the Donner Party

http://www.teleport.com/~mhaller/Primary/VReed/VReed1.html

This site features an account of the trip by Virginia Reed Murphy, a Donner Party survivor. She tells of the struggle to survive in the harsh conditions.

INDEX

ABOUT THE AUTHOR

Scott P. Werther is an editor and freelance writer from Monkton, Maryland. He spends his free moments exploring the great outdoors.